MW00902077

For Yoni and Noa, my two favorite people to gobble up.
- JDW

To Renee and Isabella, my personal art critics.
- CH

www.mascotbooks.com

If I Were Food

©2015 Jay D. Waxman. All Rights Reserved. No part of this publication may be reproduced, stored in a retrieval system or transmitted in any form by any means electronic, mechanical, or photocopying, recording or otherwise without the permission of the author.

For more information, please contact:
Mascot Books
560 Herndon Parkway #120
Herndon, VA 20170
info@mascotbooks.com

Library of Congress Control Number: 2015916257

CPSIA Code: PRT1115A
ISBN-13: 978-1-63177-139-2

Printed in the United States

IF I WERE FOOD

by Jay D. Waxman

Illustrated by Chris Herrick

If I were food,
I'd be...

A big bowl of
SPAGHETTI

Fun Fact:

The bigger an orange's navel, the sweeter it will be.

ORANGE

Tough on the outside, with vitamin-filled squishiness underneath. I'd also have a navel, which is fun to play with.

If I were food, I'd be a...

BURRITO

Frijoles = Beans
Carne = Meat
Verduras = Veggies
Queso = Cheese

Snuggled up in a big, warm tortilla blanket. Filled with beans, meats, veggies, and cheese.

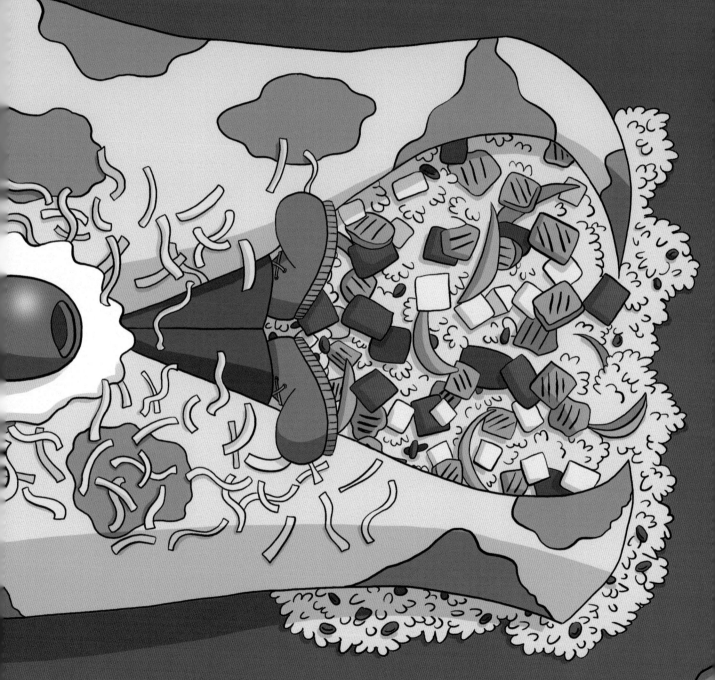

If I were food, I'd be a...

SALAD

True or False:
You can mix fruits
and vegetables in
a salad. True

Chopped, tossed, and filled with tasty crunchy things to help me grow up strong and healthy.

If I were food, I'd be a...

Soft and sweet and covered in frosting. Everyone smiles when I enter the room.

How many candles can you count? How many cherries?

If I were food, I'd be...

SUSHI

Nori = Seaweed
Wasabi = Horseradish
Kappa = Cucumber
Domo = Thank You

You need chopstick skills to take a bite of me. I'm rolled up in rice and wrapped around yummy veggies and fresh fish.

If I were food, I'd be...

I've got layers. Sometimes I'm hot. Sometimes I'm cold. Sometimes I crunch. Sometimes I don't.

If I were food, I'd be a...

I can be baked, fried, chipped, mashed, hash-browned, or pancaked. Then dipped in lots of different sauces.

If I were food, I'd be...

WATER

Fun Fact:

About 70% of the Earth is covered in water.

About the Author:

When not hanging with super villain henchmen or the minions of time, Jay is a writer and filmmaker living in Southern California, with a brilliant wife and two amazing kids.

About the Illustrator:

Chris Herrick is a children's book illustrator from Long Beach, California. Born with a paintbrush in his hand, he follows his dreams and illustrates books for kids.